9780853064527
AF593240

Best Wishes
Margaret & Reg

The Romantic Wales of Harry Secombe

in picture and song

Llyn Gwynant, Caernarvonshire

Beddgelert and the River Glaslyn

The Romantic Wales of Harry Secombe

in picture and song

Jarrold Colour Publications

Welsh Mountain Ponies

SBN 85306 452 0

Printed and bound in Great Britain by
Jarrold & Sons Limited, Norwich 173

Contents of this book

Foreword

When I was approached with the idea of compiling a book on Wales my first reaction was to shout 'Help!' Fortunately for me, Owain Arwel Hughes, the distinguished young conductor, came running to my assistance. He is a young man with all the sensitivity which is essential in his work, and possesses a knowledge of Welsh folk music and poetry far superior to mine.

His help has been invaluable, particularly because of the fact that he speaks Welsh. I have to confess that I was brought up in a part of South Wales where Welsh is not spoken at all. Having been born in Danygraig, Swansea, a stone's throw from the docks, I was more conversant at an early age with the Urdu spoken by the Indian seamen than with the Welsh language. Yet, only a few miles away, in Morriston, Welsh and English were spoken with an equal fluency. In the presence of my Welsh speaking compatriots, Sir Geraint Evans and Richard Burton, I always feel somewhat inadequate, although I have the advantage of weight on my side.

It is to my eternal regret that much of the finest Welsh poetry and drama is thus denied to me because translation, however good, blurs the impact of the original thought. Dylan Thomas, though, represents all that is best in Welsh poetry and we can read his work in undiluted form.

One doesn't have to understand the words of Welsh hymns. Just to sit in a Welsh chapel with the glorious music swirling around is enough to realise the fervour and sincerity of what is being sung.

I spent most of my boyhood in a church choir, from the time I was eight until my voice broke at the age of fourteen. At first my brother and I were in St. Stephen's Church Choir until we moved to St. Thomas's Church which was at the bottom of the street in which we lived. The drama and the music of the church services appealed to the nascent actor in me, and the church socials provided me with the opportunity to perform before an audience.

The church hall in St. Thomas's was the focal point of all social activity and my parents were deeply involved in the Passion Plays and the musical concerts produced there. My brother Fred, my sister Carol and myself were usually called in to do something at these concerts.

Strange as it may seem today, I was at first the most reluctant of the three of us, and I always remember standing on stage with the intention of reciting W. H. Davies's 'Can I forget the sweet days that have been'. I got as far as the first line and stuck, sweating, unable to remember any lines of the poem. I was gently led off stage by my brother.

This same shyness dogged me in the choir. Having to sing a solo was a frightening prospect and I would shake so much that I could hardly hold the song copy. Even at family parties or on Sunday evenings when we would all get together and sing around the piano in my grandparents' parlour I found it embarrassing to sing on my own. I would compromise by going to the outside toilet and sit there with the door open, singing bravely in the dark whilst the family would listen appreciatively and join in the chorus from inside the house. Heaven knows what the neighbours thought.

It was not until one night when I had broken my glasses playing rugby, and I had to perform a solo without them, that I found the answer to my stage fright. As I was – and still am – terribly short-sighted I could not see the audience as individuals, only as a pink amoebic mass, and my nervousness vanished.

From then on my parents could not keep me off the stage. If I had not broken my glasses that day I might be still working in the colliery office I went to after leaving school. A sobering thought – especially for the Coal Board.

Many of my favourite pieces of poetry and songs are included in this book. It is especially nice to see the words of 'God Bless the Prince of Wales' printed in full. When I was a young boy I thought 'let the prayer re-echo' was 'let the prairie echo', and I had a confused picture of cowboys standing in their stirrups, waving their stetsons and crying 'God Bless the Prince of Wales'. If they knew him, I'm sure they would!

'We'll Keep a Welcome' has particularly happy associations for me, because it was the theme song of 'Welsh Rarebit', a radio show produced at the Corey Hall in Cardiff by Mai Jones, and in which I had the privilege of playing for a year or two in the early fifties. There were great Welsh characters in the show – the late Ossie Morris, a fine comic and singer, the Tommy Trouble gang, the Lyrian Singers and all the best artists from the principality. Mai Jones was also the musical director of the show and wrote the music of 'We'll Keep a Welcome'. She helped many young artists in their early days, and it was she who first made me finish my comedy act with a song. She died some years ago and the whole of show business was the poorer for her passing.

Naturally, in a book of this description a favourite piece of music or a poem will be missed by some, but I hope that there is enough of a selection to please most people; enough to whet the appetite of the prospective visitor to Wales; to satisfy those who live in the principality; and to provide a little 'hiraeth' for those who are exiled from what is to me the most delightful place on earth – but then, I happen to be prejudiced.

HARRY SECOMBE

Introduction

HARRY SECOMBE's career, which has spanned everything from Goon humour to operatic aria, started in 1946 when he made his first professional stage appearance at London's Windmill Theatre. His act consisted of impersonations of the various ways in which people shave – but it was no joke having to shave five times a day, seven days a week. The act was a huge success at the Windmill, but did not impress a certain audience in Bolton some time later. On the first night, Harry walked off the stage at the end of the act to the sound of his own footsteps, and earned the immortal comment from the irate manager as he paid him off: 'You'll not shave in my time!' Undaunted, Harry sent the following telegram to Michael Bentine: 'AUDIENCE WITH ME ALL THE WAY STOP MANAGED TO SHAKE THEM OFF AT THE STATION.'

It was at the Windmill that Harry first started to sing. He would end his act with a duet of 'Sweetheart', singing both the baritone and falsetto parts himself. However, behind the clowning there lurked an exciting four-octave tenor voice, which was trained under the guidance of the late Maestro Manlio Di Veroli. Harry emerged from his singing lessons as one of the few bel canto tenors in Britain, and his records on the Phonogram label are consistent best-sellers.

Harry first proved his potential as an entertainer during his schooldays in his native Wales. At church socials he impersonated well-known stars of the day and on Sundays he sang in the choir. But it was not until he had worked as a pay clerk in a steel works and served throughout a war that he let his desire to be claimed by show business propel him to the Windmill Theatre and a job at £20 a week.

The rest is well-recorded history. His friendship with three other struggling comedians of that era, Peter Sellers, Spike Milligan and Michael Bentine, led to the sensationally successful radio comedy series 'The Goon Show' (once described by a BBC executive as 'that blasted "Go On" Show'), which became a national institution and still has loyal fans all over the world. From there, Harry Secombe zoomed his way to the top via radio, television, best-selling records, stage shows and films.

Highlights of the years since include a no. 1 place in the hit parade with 'This is my Song' . . . starring roles in the long-running stage musicals 'Pickwick' (in London and on Broadway) and 'The Four Musketeers' (at Drury Lane) . . . the award of the C.B.E. in 1963 for his services on behalf of the Army Benevolent Fund . . . seven Royal Command Performances . . . inclusion in the line-up of international stars at the 1970 Royal Film Performance . . . a special tribute luncheon from the Variety Club of Great Britain to mark his 25 years in show business in 1971 . . . countless TV appearances, including his own shows and 'Pickwick', both here and abroad. Key roles in many films, include 'Oliver!', 'Song of Norway', 'Doctor in Trouble' and 'Sunstruck'.

Another side of the Harry Secombe talent is currently coming to the fore – his ability as a writer. He is a member of the famous 'Punch' Round Table and a regular contributor to the magazine, and 1974 should see the publication of a book of his short stories and his first novel.

The success story of Harry Secombe goes hand in hand with an equally rewarding private life. He and his attractive wife, Myra, have been happily married since 1948 and have four children: Jennifer, Andrew, David and Katy.

The Afon Dyfi at Mallwyd, Merionethshire

Aros Mae'r Mynyddau Mawr

THE GREAT HILLS REMAIN

Ceiriog

Still the mighty mountains stand,
Round them still the tempests roar;
Still with dawn through all the land
Sing the shepherds as of yore.
Round the foot of hill and scar
Daisies still their buds unfold;
Changed the shepherds only are
On those mighty mountains old.

Passing with the passing years
Ancient customs change and flow;
Fraught with doom of joy or tears,
Generations come and go.
Out of tears' and tempests' reach
Alun Mabon sleeps secure;
Still lives on the ancient speech,
Still the ancient songs endure.

Translated by Sir H. I. Bell
Reproduced by kind permission of Collins Publishers, Glasgow

A Coracle on the River Teifi at Cenarth, Carmarthenshire

The Owls
TYLLUANOD

R. Williams Parry

When night lit up the gleaming
Of dust along the road,
And at Pen Llyn the empty bridge
The placid stream bestrode,
I heard the owls from far below
Hooting through the groves in Cwm-y-Glo.

When the wild duck rode at anchor
And rocked beneath the moon,
And the forest mere in icy spray
Across their backs was strewn,
To the wind which roared on Mynydd Du
They made their answer piteously.

When the Glaslyn slid into a shadow,
Like a sword into its sheath,
And red the mansion windows burned
The rookeries beneath,
They cried when the dogs gave cry no more,
And night came down on Ynys-for.

And when the twilight wraps creation
After its demented day,
And over worker and the work
The voiceless hush holds sway,
Their tongue will have, I promise you,
Nor joy nor pain – Too-whit, too-whoo!

Translated by David Bell
Reproduced by kind permission of Collins Publishers, Glasgow

Near Llanberis

(Letters) William Wordsworth

A little before sunset we came in sight of Llanberis Lake, Snowdon, and all the craggy hills and mountains surrounding it; the foreground a beautiful contrast to this grandeur and desolation – a green sloping hollow, furnishing a shelter for one of the most beautiful collections of lowly Welsh cottages, with thatched roofs, overgrown with plants, anywhere to be met with; the hamlet is called Cwm-y-Glo.

The Holly
Y GELYNEN

Come gentle friends let's gather round
And sing with voices merry
Praising loud the evergreen,
The tree whose name is the holly.
Fal dee roodee lam tam
Too lee riddle ee
Trilla lam tam tillam tanee
Praising loud the evergreen
The tree whose name is the holly.

This holly cannot be compared
To yew or sturdy oak tree
Nor to palace grand nor hall,
It stands alone, the holly.
Fal dee roodee lam tam
Too lee riddle ee
Trilla lam tam tillam tanee
Nor to palace grand nor hall
It stands alone, the holly.

Translated by Mary Ll. Davies
Reproduced by kind permission of
Boosey & Hawkes, Music Publishers Ltd

The picturesque village of New Quay

Penmaen Pool

Gerard Manley Hopkins

Who long for rest, who look for pleasure
Away from counter, court, or school
O where live well your lease of leisure
But here at, here at Penmaen Pool?

And all the landscape under survey,
At tranquil turns, by nature's rule,
Rides repeated topsyturvey
In frank, in fairy Penmaen Pool.

The Mawddach, how she trips! though throttled
If floodtide teeming thrills her full,
And mazy sands all water-wattled
Waylay her at ebb, past Penmaen Pool.

But what's to see in stormy weather,
When grey showers gather and gusts are cool? –
Why, raindrop-roundels looped together
That lave the face of Penmaen Pool.

Then come who pine for peace or pleasure
Away from counter, court, or school,
Spend here your measure of time and treasure
And taste the treats of Penmaen Pool.

Thou Gavest

TYDI A RODDAIST

T. Rowland Hughes

O Thou that gave the magic dawn
And sun-set, beauty bright;
O Thou that didst the Spring adorn
And gave it song and light.
Our wonder, Lord, each day restore,
And at Thy feet let us adore.

O Thou that gave the brook its song,
And to the tree its sigh,
O Thou that gave the lark, day long,
To sing its song on high;
O never let us know the days
Our hearts no longer fill with praise.

Thou who didst hear the halting tread
On Calvary's bitter way;
Thou who didst see the bloody sweat
Fall from His brow that day;
O keep us from an age that's shorn
Of sacrifice and crown of thorn.

Translated by Aneurin Talfan Davies
Reproduced by kind permission of
Christopher Davies Publishers Ltd

Affinity

CYNEFIN

T. H. Parry-Williams

To know who I am is for me quite a feat
In lush lowland fields, away from the peat.

The red in my blood has for centuries known
That all soil is not like the soil where I've grown.

But I know who I am, by a hill and a heath
And a crag, – and rushes and a lake beneath.

Reproduced by kind permission of Sir T. H. Parry-Williams

Raglan Castle, Monmouthshire

16

Nant Gwynant and Dinas Emrys, the hill beyond the stream

God Bless the Prince of Wales

Among our ancient mountains,
And from our lovely vales,
Oh! let the prayer re-echo,
'God Bless the Prince of Wales'.
With heart and voice awaken
Those minstrel strains of yore,
Till Britain's name and glory,
Resound from shore to shore!
Among our ancient mountains,
And from our lovely vales,
Oh! let the prayer re-echo,
'God Bless the Prince of Wales'.

18

The harbour from Castle Hill, Tenby

Sospan Fach

Mae bys Mary Ann wedi brifo
A Dafydd y gwas ddim yn iach,
Mae'r baban yn y crud yn crio
A'r gath wedi scrammo Johnny bach.
Sospan fach yn berwi ar y tan
Sospan fawr yn berwi ar y llawr
A'r gath wedi scrammo Johnny bach.

Land of my Fathers

HEN WLAD FY NHADAU

Evan James

Mae Hen Wlad fy Nhadau yn annwyl i mi,
Gwlad beirdd a chantorion, enwogion o fri:
Ei gwrol ryfelwyr gwladgarwyr tra mad,
Dros ryddid collasant eu gwaed.
Gwlad! Gwlad! pleidiol wyf i'm gwlad,
Tra mor yn fur
I'r bur hoff bau,
O bydded i'r heniaith barhau.

O land of my fathers the land of the free,
The home of the telyn,* so soothing to me;
Thy noble defenders were gallant and brave,
For freedom their heart's life they gave.
Wales! Wales! – home sweet home is in Wales;
Till death be passed
My love shall last,
My longing, my hiraeth for Wales.

* *harp*

The Cader Idris range overlooks Tal-y-Llyn

The Ash Grove

LLWYN ONN

Down yonder green valley where streamlets meander,
When twilight is fading I pensively rove;
Or at the bright noontide, in solitude wander,
Amid the dark shades of the lonely Ash Grove;
'Twas there, while the blackbird was cheerfully singing,
I first met that dear one the joy of my heart!
Around us for gladness the bluebells were ringing,
Ah! then little thought I how soon we should part.

Still glows the bright sunshine o'er valley and mountain,
Still warbles the blackbird its note from the tree;
Still trembles the moonbeam on streamlet and fountain,
But what are the beauties of nature to me?
With sorrow, deep sorrow, my bosom is laden,
All day I go mourning in search of my love!
Ye echoes! oh, tell me, where is the sweet maiden?
'She sleeps 'neath the green turf down by the Ash Grove'.

English words by Thos. Oliphant
Reprinted from Sing Care Away
by kind permission of Novello & Co., Ltd

Loudly Proclaim

Loudly proclaim, Wales must be free!
She is the land of liberty!
Touch not her bounds! no tyrant here shall reign!
Freedom is her right, and her freedom we'll maintain!
Come who may, none shall say
He can conqu'ror be;
For we proclaim, Wales must be free!
She is the land of liberty!

Free as the hills, free as the dales,
Free as the air is the land of Wales,
Justice her watchword, liberty her right,
None shall overcome us if firmly we unite.
Know ye all, great and small,
Victors never ye!
For we proclaim, Wales shall be free!
She is the land of liberty!

Reprinted from Sing Care Away
by kind permission of Novello & Co., Ltd

The Mountains of Glamorgan

Anon.

The mountains of Glamorgan
Look down towards the sea,
Their song is clear as any bell
In melodies that sink and swell,
And there they stand to sentinel
A land of mystery.

The mountains of Glamorgan
Grow wondrous in the spring:
Perhaps our dead folk gather there
To bless their land in song and prayer,
For every thicket, nook and lair
Is loud with whispering.

When I have reached my journey's end
And I am dead and free,
I pray that God will let me go
To wander with them to and fro
Along those singing hills I know
That look towards the sea.

Llawhaden Church by the East Cleddau River, Pembrokeshire

The mountain village of Capel Garmon

Cwm Rhondda

William Williams

Guide me, O Thou great Jehovah,
Pilgrim through this barren land;
I am weak, but Thou art mighty;
Hold me with Thy powerful hand;
  Bread of Heaven,
Feed me now and evermore.

Open now the crystal fountain,
Whence the healing stream doth flow;
Let the fiery cloudy pillar
Lead me all my journey through;
  Strong Deliverer,
Be Thou still my Strength and Shield.

When I tread the verge of Jordan,
Bid my anxious fears subside;
Death of death, and hell's Destruction,
Land me safe on Canaan's side.
  Songs of Praises
I will ever give to Thee.

Verse 1. Translated by Peter Williams
Verses 2 3 Translated by William Williams

Llyn Padarn and Snowdon

The Bells of Aberdovey

CLYCHAU ABERDYFI

Listen to the silv'ry bells
Ringing o'er the distant dells,
Ding dong, ding dong, ding dong ding,
Ring the bells of Aberdovey.
Ding dong, ding dong silv'ry bells,
Of peace and rest their chiming tells,
The bells of Aberdovey.

Ev'ry morn I wake to hear
Their welcome music pealing,
Like a fairy murmur clear,
Within my window stealing,
'Ope your eyes', they seem to say,
'Rise to greet another day,
Ready for your work and play',
Ring the bells of Aberdovey.

When the happy day is done,
'Work is over, rest is won,
Go to slumber with the sun',
Ring the bells of Aberdovey.
Ding dong, ding dong, silv'ry bells,
Of peace and rest their chiming tells,
The bells of Aberdovey.

When in far off lands I roam,
My thoughts are homeward straying,
In my heart the bells of home
Their melody are playing.
'Be of cheer', they say to me,
'In your home beyond the sea,
They are thinking too of thee',
Say the bells of Aberdovey.

Reprinted from Sing Care Away
by kind permission of Novello & Co., Ltd

Berwyn

Robert Ellis (Cynddelw)

On Berwyn's heights to wander
And breathe there the summer air
I'd haste, and on the barest
Of the lone summits I'd rest.

Fair blossoms of the mountain
Sweetest odours bring again;
Softest voices fill the hill,
Grasshopper sounds commingle.

And ever with sweet murmurs
The bees seek the honey'd flow'rs
Happy birds in sunny air
Sing their melodies tender;
While upward in the sunlight
The lark trills in heaven's height.

O Happy morn of glory,
Morning of joy bright and free,
My happy morn of childhood,
White as frost in winter rude.

Now I'm old the snows begin,
O my longing for Berwyn,
I who did nigh forget thee
Awak'ning love would praise thee.

After all this world may win,
Let me slumber in Berwyn;
Could a grave be given me,
In Berwyn down I'd lay me;
To my door and to my land,
I'll go back to my homeland
And Berwyn, high and gloomy,
My gravestone shall ever be,
And stormwinds shall ever blow
In fury o'er my pillow.

The River Ystwyth on the road from Rhayader to Devil's Bridge

Captain Morgan

Ceiriog

Gird to your armour father's shining sword;
Fight for your country my young lord!
Like smoke from hamlets rising to the sky,
All your companions answer the cry.
Wipe the tears, to your saddle spring,
Hear the hissing arrows like serpents sing;
Draw your longbow, let your arm be strong,
Glory to your father, renowned in song!

Spur to the battle, show your standard, go,
Raise the red banner against the foe!
Blow on your trumpet, let it split his ear,
See him retreating, filled with fear.
Hark my hero, for the joyful cry:
'We have won the battle', is wafted high;
Take my blessing, go in Heaven's name,
Glory to your father, who knew not shame!

Translated and reproduced by kind permission of W. Eifion Powell

The River Dee at Llangollen

Watching the White Wheat

BUGEILIO'R GWENITH GWYN

Wil Hopcyn

I am a foolish loving swain,
Upset by fancy's notion,
Another man has gleaned the grain,
I tended with devotion;
O! why my fair, young, lovely maid!
Will you not walk beside me?
Your growing beauty does not fade,
And fairer still, I find thee.

Translated and reproduced by kind permission of W. Eifion Powell

Men of Harlech

Ceiriog

See the beacon brightly burning,
Hark the fiery voices shouting,
For the mighty to come fighting,
Bravely at the call.
To the clarions of the Princes,
Sounds of combat, strangers' voices,
And the charging of the horses,
All the rocks shall fall.
Arfon's undefeated,
Let the song be sounded,
Wales will fight for freedom yet,
For greatness amongst nations.
In the beacon's white light burning,
Hear the dying hero's moaning:
'Freedom's voice is ever calling
For the best men all'.

Never shall the foeman beat us,
Men of Harlech, they'll protect us;
And the mighty Lord who frees us,
Puts our foes to flight.
See the armies of our captains,
All descending from the mountains!
Like a hundred hurtling fountains
Dancing in their might!
May our leaders flourish!
And our haters perish!
As within their hearts they feel
The sharpness of our spirit;
Sword at sword will still be striking,
Steel to steel will still be sounding,
Gwalia's flag, I see it rising,
Freedom wins the fight!

Translated and reproduced by kind permission of W. Eifion Powell

Tintern Abbey, created in the Twelfth century

Tintern Abbey

William Wordsworth
(Lines composed a few miles above Tintern Abbey, on revisiting the banks of the Wye during a tour, July 13, 1798)

Five years have passed; five summers, with the length
Of five long winters! and again I hear
These waters, rolling from their mountain-springs
With a sweet inland murmur. – Once again
Do I behold those steep and lofty cliffs,
Which on a wild secluded scene impress
Thoughts of more deep seclusion: and connect
The landscape with the quiet of the sky.

Remembrance

COFIO

Waldo Williams

One blissful moment as the sun is setting,
A mellow moment ere the night comes on,
To bring to mind things which are long forgotten,
Now lost in dust of eras that are gone.

Now like the foam breaking on lonely beaches,
Or the wind's song and no one there to hear,
I know they call on us in vain to listen, –
The old forgotten things men loved so dear.

Things wrought through cunning skill in early ages,
Neat little dwellings and resplendent halls,
And well-told stories that are lost for ever,
And olden gods on whom no suppliant calls.

The little words of languages once living,
Lively was then their sound on lips of men,
And pleasing to the ear in children's prattle,
But now, no tongue will fashion them again.

O countless generations of earth's children,
Of dreams divine, and fragile godlikeness,
Is there but stillness for the hearts that quickened,
That knew delight and knew grief's bitterness?

Often when evening falls and I am lonely
I long once more to bring you all to mind,
Pray, is there no-one treasures and holds dear
The old forgotten things of humankind?

Translated by D. M. Lloyd
Reproduced by kind permission of Collins Publishers, Glasgow

St. Govan

Dr. J. Morgan Lloyd

St. Govan, he built him a cell
By the side of the Pembroke sea,
And there, as the crannied sea-gulls dwell,
In a tiny, secret citadel
He sighed for eternity.

St. Govan, he built him a cell
Between the wild sky and the sea,
Where the sunsets redden the rolling swell
And brooding splendour has thrown her spell
On valley and moorland lea.

St. Govan still lies in his cell,
But his soul, long since, is free
And one may wonder – and who can tell –
If good St. Govan likes Heaven as well
As his cell by that sounding sea?

Reproduced by kind permission of
The Gwynn Publishing Co., Llangollen, N. Wales

Falls on the Mellte River, near Ystradfellte, Breconshire

Llyn Ogwen lies in the beautiful Nant Ffrancon Pass

My Love is a Venus

MAE 'NGHARIAD I'N FENWS

My dear one is slender
And bright as the morn,
My dear one is fairer
Than rose on the thorn;
As Venus, her beauty,
So comely her youth,
I am not commending
I speak but the truth.

O dear little maiden
The fairest, I trow,
With teeth, oh so dainty
And cheeks all aglow;
Her two eyes, so smiling
Her twin brows so fine,
Oh, how I would love her,
If I knew she'd be mine!

Translated by D. Vaughan Thomas
Reprinted from Ten Welsh Folk Songs *by kind permission of The Gwynn Publishing Co., Llangollen, N. Wales*

38

Dolwyddelan Castle, Caernarvonshire

Where can my loved one be?

PA LE MAE 'NGHARIAD I?

Where can my loved one be?
Oh! is there none who knows?
Where can my loved one be?
The night begins to close.
No sound of footsteps can be heard,
Where can my loved one be?
I never knew her break her word,
Where can my loved one be?

Translated by Sir H. I. Bell
Reprinted from Eleven Welsh Folk Songs *by kind permission of The Gwynn Publishing Co., Llangollen, N. Wales*

The Loom

Y GWYDD

As I about sunsetting,
At the loom,
Toiled on all else forgetting,
At the loom,
A thought, the silence breaking,
Set all my heart a-quaking;
Is this my last endeavour,
At the loom,
Ere I must part for ever
From the loom?

Translated by Sir H. I. Bell
Reprinted from Old Welsh Folk Songs *by kind permission of The Gwynn Publishing Co., Llangollen, N. Wales*

Conway Castle

Fair Lisa

LISA LAN

Full many a time I came to woo,
Oft, Lisa, came a-courting you;
I kissed your lips when we did meet,
No honey ever was so sweet!

My dainty branch, my only dear,
No woman comes your beauty near;
'Tis you who with my passion play,
'Tis you who steals my life away.

Whene'er at eve I walk apart,
Like wax will melt my lovesick heart;
And but to hear the small birds sing,
The longing to my soul will bring.

Ah, will you come to bid good-bye,
When in the earth my form must lie?
I hope you too will there be found,
When men shall lay me in the ground.

Translated by Sir H. I. Bell
Reprinted from Un ar ddeg o Ganeuon Gwerin Cymru
by kind permission of The Gwynn Publishing Co.,
Llangollen, N. Wales

White Rose of Summer

LLIW GWYN RHOSYN YR HAF

Richard Williams (Dic Dywyll)

'A fair good morrow, lovely maiden,
White wild rose of my heart!
For you my soul is sorrow-laden,
White wild rose of my heart!'
'Nay, cease, dull oaf, your idle chatter,
The silliest babble ever I heard!
You and your oaths are no great matter –
That's truth in a single word!'

'Your kiss is sweeter far than honey,
White wild rose of my heart!
Such nectar ne'er was bought for money,
White wild rose of my heart!'
'And yours, for all your fond devotion,
The silliest babble ever I heard!
As loathsome as a doctor's potion –
That's truth in a single word!'

'Ah me! salt tears, you'll still be flowing,
White wild rose of my heart!
But kiss me once and I'll be going,
White wild rose of my heart!'
'Oh no, my love, I cannot grieve you,
A tenderer speech you never have heard!
I gave you two, fifteen I'll give you –
That's truth in a single word!'

Translated by Sir H. I. Bell
Reprinted from Old Welsh Folk Songs *by kind permission of The Gwynn Publishing Co., Llangollen, N. Wales*

In Pontypridd is my lover

YM MHONTYPRIDD MAE 'NGHARIAD

At Pontypridd I'd meet her,
At Pontypridd would greet her,
At Pontypridd would make her mine,
Was never maiden sweeter.

Of songs I've heard a many,
Have seen as much as any
Of dainty sights and maidens fair,
But none so rare as Jenny.

My cot beside the river,
My brindled kine I'll give her,
My farm by Taff, a loving heart,
And we'll not part for ever.

Translated by Sir H. I. Bell
Reprinted from 20 Alaw Gymreig *by kind permission of The Gwynn Publishing Co., Llangollen, N. Wales*

43

The Pass of Aberglaslyn

44

The Bwlch Oerddrws Pass at Dinas Mawddwy, Merionethshire

There is my sweetheart

DACW 'NGHARIAD I LAWR YN Y BERLLAN

There's my love in the orchard yonder
Too rum dee ro rum dee raddle iddle al,
Oh that I with her might wander
Too rum dee ro rum dee raddle iddle al,
There's the house and barn so roomy,
There's the door it beckons to me.
Fal dee raddle iddle al
Fal dee raddle iddle al
Too rum dee ro rum dee raddle iddle al.

Mountain paths among the heather,
One is better far than other;
And there ways by brook and hollow,
Deep as maiden's mind to follow.

There's the harp, but nought can cheer me,
For my love is never near me;
If her mind I can't discover,
What can I, her hapless lover?

All my love to her is given,
And my heart is nearly riven;
This has brought her, too, I'm learning,
Tears for me, and sighs, and yearning.

Translated by D. Vaughan Thomas
Reprinted from Ten Welsh Folk Songs *by kind permission of The Gwynn Publishing Co., Llangollen, N. Wales*

Caernarvon Castle

By the Sea

AR LAN Y MOR

Down by the sea are deep red roses,
Down by the sea are pure white lilies,
Down by the sea my love is dwelling
And sleeps by night and wakes at morning.

Down by the sea are bluish pebbles,
Down by the sea are silver brambles,
Down by the sea is truth excelling,
Down by the sea my love is dwelling.

Translated by W. S. Gwynn Williams
Reproduced by kind permission of
The Gwynn Publishing Co., Llangollen, N. Wales

While there's salt within the sea

TRA BO DWR Y MOR YN HALLT

Wil Hopcyn

While there's salt within the sea,
And life in me to bless me;
While a heart within me beats,
Your love will sure possess me.

You each day I fairer see,
Or love in me grows stronger;
For His dear sake who made you fair,
O spare to plague me longer.

Translated by Sir H. I. Bell
Reprinted from Eleven Welsh Folk Songs *by kind permission*
of The Gwynn Publishing Co., Llangollen, N. Wales

48

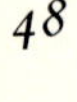

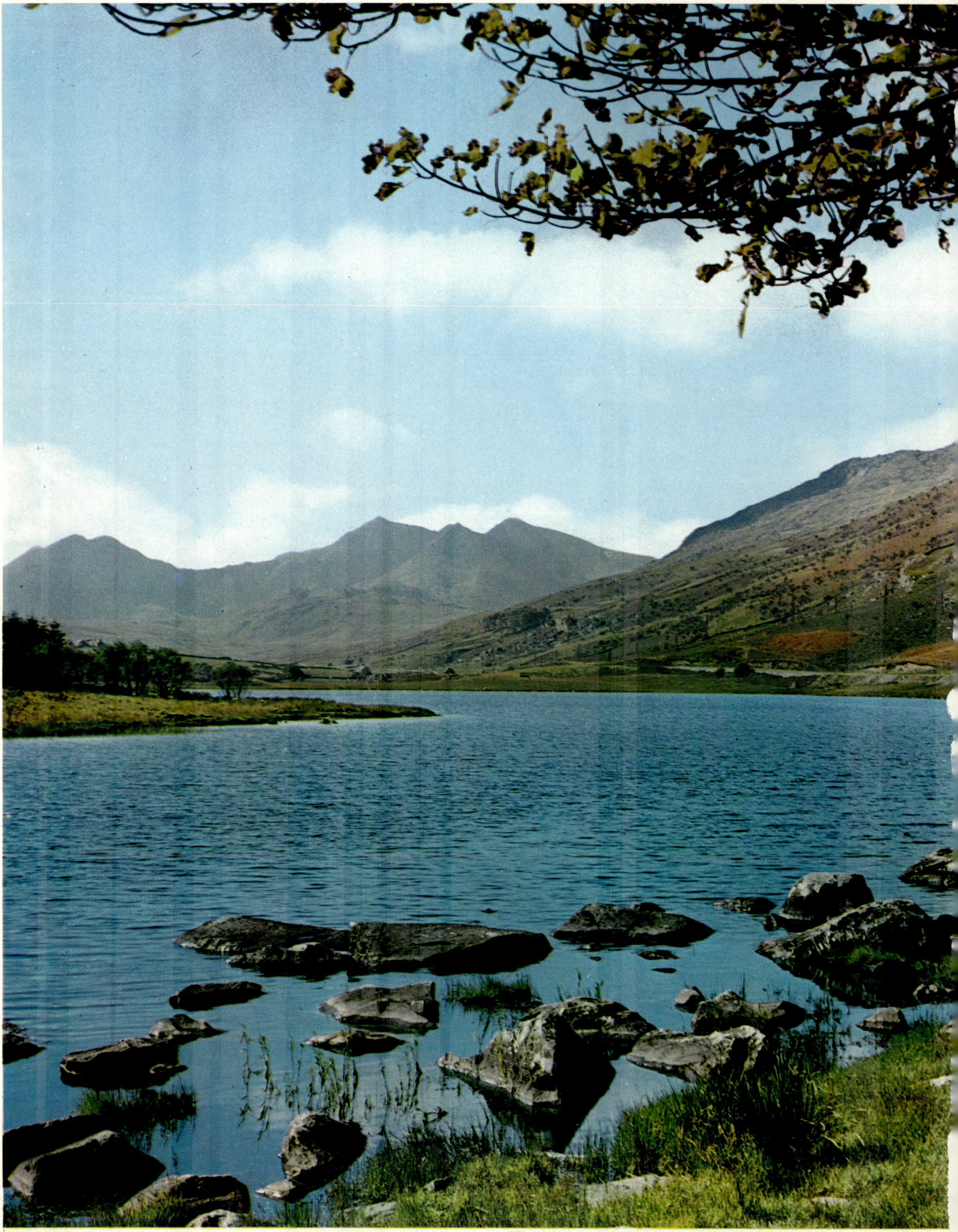

Lovely Llyn Mymber and Snowdon

The Dove

Y GLOMEN

As I one day at my good pleasure
Walked through the woodland at my leisure,
Above my head I heard a dove call,
A-making moan, 'Alone, Alone!
Where is my lover?'

Then nearer still I went and nearer,
That I might hear her words the clearer,
And closer yet, and then I asked her,
The loveliest bird I ever heard,
What was it vexed her?

'O gentle dove, O cease repining,
The sun once more will soon be shining,
The trees their leafy dress revealing;
Remember, dear, when summer's here,
The hawks come stealing'.

Translated by Sir. H. I. Bell
Reproduced by kind permission of
The Gwynn Publishing Co., Llangollen, N. Wales

Days that have been

W. H. Davies

Can I forget the sweet days that have been,
When poetry first began to warm my blood;
When from the hills of Gwent I saw the earth
Burned into two by Severn's silver flood:

When I would go alone at night to see
The moonlight, like a big white butterfly,
Dreaming on that old castle near Caerleon,
While at its side the Usk went softly by:

When I would stare at lovely clouds in Heaven,
Or watch them when reported by deep streams;
When feeling pressed like thunder, but would not
Break into that grand music of my dreams?

Can I forget the sweet days that have been,
The villages so green that I have been in;
Llantarnam, Magor, Malpas and Llanwern,
Liswery, old Caerleon, and Alteryn?

Can I forget the banks of Malpas Brook,
Or Ebbw's voice in such a wild delight,
As on he dashed with pebbles in his throat,
Gurgling towards the sea with all his might?

Ah, when I see a leafy village now,
I sigh and ask it for Llantarnam's green;
I ask each river where is Ebbw's voice –
In memory of the sweet days that have been.

The River Severn

This is the morning bright and clear,
To stand on top of Christchurch Hill;
We'll see the Severn, looking down,
In all his silver beauty, Love –
Where he lies basking in the sun.

My lovely Severn shines as bright
As any moon on trucks of coal,
Or sun above our greenest meadow;
Till I again defy the world
To search his face and find a shadow.

Kidwelly Castle, Carmarthenshire

The village of Llanfrothan near Portmadoc

Rev. Eli Jenkins' Prayer

UNDER MILK WOOD

Dylan Thomas

Dear Gwalia! I know there are
Towns lovelier than ours,
And fairer hills and loftier far,
And groves more full of flowers.

And boskier woods more blithe with spring
And bright with birds' adorning,
And sweeter bards than I to sing
Their praise this beauteous morning.

By Cader Idris, tempest-torn,
Or Moel yr Wyddfa's glory,
Carnedd Llewellyn beauty born,
Plinlimmon old in story.

By mountains where King Arthur dreams,
By Penmaenmawr defiant,
Llaregyb Hill a molehill seems,
A pygmy to a giant.

A tiny dingle is Milk Wood,
By Golden Grove 'neath Grongar,
But let me choose and oh! I should
Love all my life and longer

To stroll among our trees and stray
In Goosegog Lane, on Donkey Down,
And hear the Dewi sing all day,
And never, never leave the town.

The Cliffs and South Stack Lighthouse, Holy Island, Anglesey

New Year's Eve

NOS GALAN

Now the joyful bells a-ringing,
All ye mountains, praise the Lord!
Lift our hearts like birds a-winging,
All ye mountains, praise the Lord!
Now our festal season, bringing
Kinsmen all to bide and board,
Sets our cheery voices ringing:
All ye mountains, praise the Lord!

Dear our home as dear none other;
Where the mountains praise the Lord!
Gladly here our care we smother;
Where the mountains praise the Lord!
Here we know that Christ our brother
Binds us all as by a chord:
He was born of Mary, mother,
Where the mountains praise the Lord!

Cold the year, new whiteness wearing,
All ye mountains, praise the Lord!
Peace, goodwill to us a-bearing,
All ye mountains, praise the Lord!
Now we all God's goodness sharing
Break the bread and sheathe the sword:
Bright our hearts the signal flaring,
All ye mountains, praise the Lord!

Reproduced from Oxford Book of Carols *by kind permission of the Oxford University Press*

The Angry Summer

extract from
Idris Davies

Look at the valleys down there in the darkness,
Long bracelets of twinkling lights,
And here with the mountain breeze on your brow
Consider the folk in the numberless streets
Between the long dark ridges, north to south.
Township after township lit up in long broken lines,
Silent and sparkling, sprinkling with jewels the night,
. . . . . .
. . . . . .
And one by one the lights shall go out
In all the valleys, leaving isolated lamps, silver pins,
Sticking into the inverted velvet of the midnight air.
And you shall listen then to the silence
That is not silence, to the murmur
Of the uneasy centuries among the ancient hills and valleys
As here you stand with the mountain breeze on your brow.

Reproduced by kind permission of Mrs Dorothy Morris and Faber & Faber

56

Picton Castle, near Haverfordwest, Pembrokeshire

Arfon

Idris Davies

All this rugged land is sacred
And its glory shall not die,
Where the mountains meet the Menai,
Where Eryri cleaves the sky.

Here of old the harp and bugle
Stirred the fettered to be free,
And the wild winds waved the banners
That led to pride and liberty.

Here of old the blazing torches
Thrilled the heart and thrilled the eye,
Where the mountains meet the Menai,
Where Eryri cleaves the sky.

Here, this eve, the shores are quiet
And all Arfon seems at rest,
And we with dreams can but remember
Those whose days with deeds were blest.

Still those warriors wage *our* battles
And their voices shall not die
Where the mountains meet the Menai,
Where Eryri cleaves the sky.

Still a golden language triumphs
On these mountains by the sea,
And I heard a child this morning
Sing of Glyndwrs yet to be.

Reproduced by kind permission of
Mrs Dorothy Morris and Faber & Faber

Rhymney

Idris Davies

When April came to Rhymney
With shower and sun and shower,
The green hills and the brown hills
Could sport some simple flower,
And sweet it was to fancy
That even the blackest mound
Was proud of its single daisy
Rooted in bitter ground.

And old men would remember
And young men would be vain,
And the hawthorn by the pithead
Would blossom in the rain,
And the drabbest streets of evening,
They had their magic hour,
When April came to Rhymney
With shower and sun and shower.

Reproduced by kind permission of
Mrs Dorothy Morris and Faber & Faber

David of the White Rock
DAFYDD Y GARREG WEN

Ceiriog

David the Bard for his harp softly cried
'Let me in dying have thee by my side.
Let my weak fingers caress thee once more
God bless my loved ones till life's song be o'er'

Last night an angel called softly to me –
'David, come home now and play with the free'.
Harp of my fathers, my song now must cease;
God bless my loved ones and grant them His peace.

Translated by Douglas Llewellyn
Reproduced by kind permission of
Boosey & Hawkes, Music Publishers Ltd

Portmeirion, Merionethshire

The Valley of the Dee, Denbighshire

We'll Keep a Welcome

Far away a voice is calling
Bells of memory chime
Come home again, come home again,
They call through the oceans of time.
We'll keep a welcome in the hillside;
We'll keep a welcome in the vales,
This land you knew will still be singing
When you come home again to Wales;
This land of song will keep a welcome
And with a love that never fails,
We'll kiss away each hour of hiraeth,
When you come home again to Wales.

Reproduced by kind permission of Lawrence Wright Music Co. Ltd

Pen-y-cwm from Pont Aber Geiwr, Merioneth

All through the night
AR HYD Y NOS

Ceiriog

Ev'ry star in heaven is singing
All through the night,
Hear the glorious music ringing
All through the night
Songs of sweet ethereal lightness
Wrought in realms of peace and whiteness;
See, the dark gives way to brightness
All through the night.

Look, my love, the stars are smiling
All through the night,
Lighting, soothing and beguiling
Earth's sombre plight:
So, when age brings grief and sorrow,
From each other we can borrow
Faith in our sublime tomorrow,
All through the night.

Translated by A. G. Prys-Jones
Reprinted from Songs of Wales *by kind permission of*
Boosey & Hawkes, Music Publishers Ltd

Farewell to the Parish of Llangower
FFARWEL I BLWY LLANGOWER

Farewell to old Llangower,
And Bala dear, farewell,
And her I love so truly,
Whose name I cannot tell;
I'm bound away for England,
All sad at heart and dumb,
To join the dance and singing,
Playing, marching before the drum.

From out the heather stealing
The gentle stream tiptoes,
Its farewell music pealing
As down the dale it goes;
I too must go must wander
Where none can play for me,
That rivers' flowing chorus,
That magical melody.

A moment let me linger,
The winding lanes along,
Remembering eaves of winter
That we would gild with song;
That here in times hereafter
My thoughts may ever come,
And bring from lands of exile
My heart and my hiraeth home.

Verse 1. Translated by D. Vaughan Thomas
Reprinted from Ten Welsh Folk Songs *by kind permission of*
The Gwynn Publishing Co., Llangollen, N. Wales

64

Caswell Bay, Glamorgan